SCHALK'S LITTLE BOOK ON
SPIRITUAL MATURITY

ALSO BY SCHALK HOLLOWAY

NOVELS

The Brooklyn Saga:
Disciple's Fault
Brother's Request

The Posterity Doctrine:
Novus Dies (A New Day)

SUBJECT LITERATURE

Die Groot Storie (SCM)
The Maul Book (co-authored with Gavin Coleman)

The Little Book Series:
Schalk's Little Book on Fundamentals (The Black Book)
Schalk's Little Book of Combative Principles (The White Book)
Schalk's Little Book for Brothers (The Red Book)
Schalk's Little Book on Spiritual Maturity (The Gold Book)

ILLUSTRATED (NOT CHILDREN BOOKS)

Schalk's Occasionally 'Terribyly' Illustrated Prodding Absurdity

SCHALK'S LITTLE BOOK ON

SPIRITUAL

MATURITY

WHY THE CHURCH SHOULD FORGET ABOUT LEADERSHIP

—AT LEAST FOR A WHILE.

Schalk Holloway

Dedicated to the Bride, with love.

CONTENTS

INTRODUCTION

Hebrews 5:12 (ESV) 12 For though by this time you ought to be…

For the last couple of decades, both in the world and the church, we have seen a tremendous focus on leadership. Books, courses, workshops, programs, and sermons on the topic abound. We live in a time where there is no shortage on leadership focused content. However, upon closer scrutiny, we also live in a time where leaders struggle to go the distance: sinfulness and moral failure hampers the church leadership's testimony and efficacy; lack of resiliency and clinical burnout leads to a loss in momentum and unfortunate, unhealthy employee and member turnover.

I would even venture an observation as objective truth: Most serious moral and resiliency related failures and challenges only surface after a church member has been given some sort of leadership responsibility.

Why does that happen one might ask? Well, a better leading question might be: why did we trust the member with leadership responsibilities in the first place? At the risk of offending, let me hazard an over generalised summation of most churches' lay and volunteer recruitment processes: first, the member consistently attended church services and programs; second, the member seems to be a swell guy or gal; third, the member lay somewhere on the spectrum of being open to instruction or downright ambitious; four, they may or may not have attended certain required training or discipleship.

Let's assume my summation is accurate. We now recruit the member and give them some form of responsibility, only to find things derailing a couple of months later. There are obvious exceptions to this phenomenon but the sad reality is that it happens more frequently than which we would like to admit.

Another good question might be: is there Biblical example of the phenomenon of moral failure and resiliency challenges within leadership? The answer is yes, there are clear Biblical examples, but it does seem like the Biblical ratio is far healthier than the contemporary church's. Also, the Biblical example seems to show that most that have 'occasional' failures or breakdowns—think David and Bathsheba, Elijah wanting to die, or Moses telling the Lord to rather kill him—eventually dust themselves off and continue to execute the responsibilities that they have been entrusted with. In the contemporary church, for the most part, we lose that member to our congregation and sometimes even to the church. In the wake of their departure, much dismay and destruction is frequently left behind.

The pattern seems to be clear: the church is struggling to determine who is objectively ready for leadership responsibilities. Because of this lack of understanding, the church is also struggling to effectively prepare members for lifelong service in the Body.

Sadly, some will read this and only question the church member's salvation and dedication to Jesus. However, I argue that it's more likely that every local congregation eventually ends up harvesting what their elders sow. As leaders ourselves, we are utterly responsible for our approach to discipling and developing the next generation. I would further argue, that it is only after we have done all that we can from our side, that can we can stand back and say, 'Okay, maybe that member simply doesn't want to.'

Which leads me to the critical question from which this Little Book was born, 'How accurate is our current Biblical understanding of general Christian and leadership development?' This Little Book would like to offer concise insight and strategy with which to reconsider the answer. My prayer is that its principles will lead you and your congregation into a fresh season of stability and consistency, as well as the phenomenal growth that flows from these two.

STANDARDS

Ephesians 4:11-14 (ESV) 11 And he gave the apostles, the prophets, the evangelists, the shepherds and teachers, 12 to equip the saints for the work of ministry, for building up the body of Christ, 13 until we all attain to the unity of the faith and of the knowledge of the Son of God, to mature manhood, to the measure of the stature of the fullness of Christ, 14 so that we may no longer be children, tossed to and fro by the waves and carried about by every wind of doctrine, by human cunning, by craftiness in deceitful schemes.

The fivefold ministry—or whatever your specific denominational background calls them—were always intended as the means to an end. Christ gave them to the church so that they could work a specific outcome. His plan was that they, through their individual and collective mandate, gifts, and efforts, would take the church and intentionally lead them in a specific direction and towards a specific goal. We see clearly in Paul's consideration of himself, how it was never Christ's intention that we elevate, or focus on, the positional status of these roles; whereas the fivefold ministry is functionally required for the church to flourish, it's simply not about them.

Their work, or rather, Christ's expectation of them, is that they would bring the church to a place of maturity. Note first, that Paul specifically says 'until we all attain', which means that each and every member of the church should individually reach maturity. Obviously, this would lead to a mature collective Body, but the Biblical focus is clearly on the individual. We could paraphrase and say that, 'Christ gave us the fivefold ministry so that they could bring each and every member of His church to individual maturity.'

Paul provides us with the end–goal, which is maturity, and then goes on to unpack some of its qualifiers. The list of qualifiers for maturity isn't ordered qualitatively, it's simply a list. 'Mature manhood' is set as being one with the 'unity of faith', having the 'knowledge of the Son of God', and 'not being tossed around to and fro by the waves and carried about by every wind of doctrine, by human cunning, by craftiness in deceitful schemes.' It is important to note, though, that Paul clearly states that we should aim for, becoming mature equal to, 'the measure of the stature of the fullness of Christ'.

Simply said, each individual member of the church is called to reach the same level of maturity as Christ Himself.

It would be interesting to assess how many members of the church would even believe this to be possible. Large parts of the Body of Christ struggle with the idea that we can compare, or aim for, or attain, or be on par with Christ when it comes to any facet of our spiritual lives. Paul says, in Romans 8:29, that 'those whom he foreknew he also predestined to be conformed to the image of his Son, in order that he might be the firstborn among many brothers.' Ah, the detractor would say, but that is only true when considering God's view of us, it can not be true in any other way. However, I could easily argue that the detractor's Scriptural interpretation relates more to how they see themselves than to Biblical truth. How easily we forget that upon salvation we are taken from the bloodline of Adam and placed in the bloodline of Christ, our older brother. We are, in many ways, cut from the same rock as Him.

What is true, though, is that we could never match Him in His mandate and destiny. Vocationally, there was always only meant to be one Messiah and Christ, and that was Jesus, the incarnated Son of God. As such, it should be evident that we cannot be His equal in terms of His unique identity and calling, in the same way that you and I cannot be the equals of Paul, Peter, or John's unique identities or callings. However, Scripture clearly shows that we are each called to mature unto the same 'measure of the the stature of the fullness of Christ.'

Here's the rub: compare the focus and resources spent on leadership within the church, to that of bringing each and every member to spiritual maturity, and we quickly realise how out of balance the equation is. Isn't it strange that most churches discuss, plan and program for, and invest resources into the singular gift of leadership, but so few are focused on developing spiritual maturity in their members? Granted, it might be argued that it's the underlying purpose of whatever the elders are trying to achieve within their congregation, which is to mean that it's tacitly assumed rather than explicitly stated. To which I humbly argue: nonsense. If we are not even using or discussing the term 'spiritual maturity' and what it entails, how can we aim for it with a laser–like focus?

Furthermore, someone might ask why this thing called 'maturity' is so important? Paul answers clearly: 'so that we may no longer be children, tossed to and fro by the waves and carried about by every wind of doctrine, by human cunning, by craftiness in deceitful schemes.'

Spiritual maturity brings stability and consistency into the Body. The spiritually mature man, or woman, is able to weather the storm, to fight off the enemy, and to carry the loads of others. There's a reason I'm referring to it as spiritual maturity:

it is to do so in contrast with regular or emotional maturity. Spiritual maturity is 'its own thing' and we'll unpack that later.

However, let's borrow from emotional maturity for a moment. Emotional maturity can be defined as 'acting based on a predetermined value system'. For example, if respectful conversation is a value, we don't give over to destructive outbursts; if honesty is a value, we don't lie when feeling certain types of pressures; etc. The emotionally mature person is able to maintain their values in the face of opposing or aggravating stimulus.

Even though spiritual maturity is a dynamic apart, it would be helpful for now think of it in the same way as emotional maturity. The spiritually mature person is stable and consistent. It is the person that we can build with and on. It is the person that can take responsibility in the Body and, regardless of opposing or aggravating stimulus, execute on that responsibility for extended periods of time. It is for this reason that this Little Book argues strongly for the primacy of spiritual maturity above leadership. We are called and mandated by Christ to ensure that each and every member of the Body reaches mature manhood. Only then should we become overly concerned with individual gifts and callings.

Leaders are not failing due to a lack of leadership training, leaders are failing due to a lack of spiritual maturity.

URGENCY

Hebrews 5:12 (ESV) For though by this time you ought to be teachers, you need someone to teach you again the basic principles of the oracles of God. You need milk, not solid food,

1 Corinthians 3:1-3 (ESV) 1 But I, brothers, could not address you as spiritual people, but as people of the flesh, as infants in Christ. 2 I fed you with milk, not solid food, for you were not ready for it. And even now you are not yet ready, 3 for you are still of the flesh. For while there is jealousy and strife among you, are you not of the flesh and behaving only in a human way?

The writer of Hebrews presumes that there is a timeframe connected to maturing. In his mind, his readers should have been able to consume solid food, a sure sign of having grown out of infancy, 'by this time'.

Focus on this singular issue: Biblically there is an expectation that we should mature by a certain time.

Yes, aspects of our lives will be maturing until the day we die, but a certain level of maturity is expected by both the writer of Hebrews and Paul within a certain period of time. In the minds of these two writers, there is no room for remaining in spiritual infancy in perpetuity.

Apart from the clear expectation, it is also important to note the tone of both writers: they are writing from tangible frustration. They are not at peace with their readers' lingering immaturity. In tone, it is clear that they are admonishing their readers in a most firm manner. The root of this frustration is the same as for any contemporary church elder: all members should at some stage take up their individual responsibilities to the church, but many don't. Whereas the readers of these letters should be ministering by now, instead, they are still keeping themselves busy with the mundanities of fleshly living. They are still immature and thus impossible to build with and on.

What does this mean to the reader of this Little Book? It should be evident that the writer of Hebrews, as well as Paul, sees a clear connection between spiritual maturity and the works of the ministry. It is understood by them that a level of maturity is required for the church to be effective. This is why they are focused on the theme of maturity in the first place.

Referring back to Ephesians 4:11-13 one might argue that no, actually works come before maturity. This is an astute observation that requires an appropriate explanation: there is a difference between active service and assuming responsibility within the church. Whereas anyone can help out, not everyone should be entrusted with responsibility. To become a teacher, as in Hebrews 5:12, is to be entrusted with the very lives of the sheep. As such, yes, a part of the road to maturity leads through the discipline of active service, through helping where and as needed, but it does not in any way relate to receiving responsibility. The writer in Hebrews is impressing on the readers that they should by now be ready and trustworthy to bear the weight of responsibility, but that due to their immaturity they simply aren't.

Isn't it strange then that we seldom see or hear of this urgency in the contemporary church? We see the need, most definitely. By God's grace I have a long history in various forms of ministry, and I've sat through many lamentful conversations where the need for more volunteers, 'leaders', and ministers was thoroughly discussed. Plans were made, programs were implemented: increase the volunteer group to increase the pool of potential leaders, that'll solve our problems!

However, here we still are, having the same conversations. I'll hazard a guess why: because we have no urgent focus on spiritual maturity. The church has all but forgotten that it is the mature believer on which the Body is built. It is the mature believer that has what the immature believer needs. It is the mature believer that will hold strong and fast when the storm hits. It is the mature believer that invests in others and raises them up, without even having to be asked to do so.

The mature believer both understands and is able to consistently deliver what the church requires. This is why the writer of Hebrews and Paul are frustrated: they want the readers to wake up and step into maturity so that the Body might benefit.

An interesting rabbit hole one might attempt is that of the timeframe itself. Is it possible to determine how long this measure of maturity will take to develop? Whereas it might be possible to ascertain a timeframe through diligent research, I'm not convinced that it would be useful. However, certain principles can be found in the Word.

We see in 1 Timothy 3:6 Paul's instruction to Timothy appoint elders. Elders, within the church environment, carry responsibility. Paul clearly states that elders should not be new believers, or recent converts, as they might become proud and susceptible to attacks by the devil. Paul understands that a certain level of maturity is required for a person to be able to ward off fleshly and demonic attacks. The new believer, or infant in Christ, has not yet developed that resiliency.

If we refer back to Hebrews 5 it's evident that there are certain doctrinal elements that should be established within the believer. Sound doctrine is tremendously important as it forms a large part of the believer's defense against attack. I'm reminded of my early years in ministry: after exhausting my teachable topics I turned to a brother and asked him what I should now teach? He simply said, 'Start again from the beginning.' The wisdom lies in understanding that maturity comes from mastering sound doctrine, and that this is achieved by the repetition of the fundamentals, and not being addicted to a constant flow of new revelations.

Furthermore, we see in Ephesians 4:11-13 that 'service experience' within the Body develops maturity. Active service, whether in the mundane or the specialised, places the believer within an environment where they are forced to learn, adapt, and grow. Many times it is through the feedback loop provided by active service that one can best disciple, mentor, and develop new believers. Again, and I can't stress it enough, I am not referring to loading new converts with ministry responsibility, but simply granting them opportunities to serve and minister under the covering of mature believers.

So, in essence, three things are required for maturing: time, teaching, and service experience within the church. We see these elements being present when considering the apostles' (including Paul's) own developmental journeys. We could even venture a broad timeframe based on their paths to maturity: it seems like a couple of years of investment and growth, at the very least, might be what's needed. Not months, and not decades, but a couple of years of focused development at the very least.

Contrast this 'couple of years' with how quickly and easily we hand out responsibility in the church and it should become evident why so many members and leaders struggle to go the distance. Furthermore, when you consider the Biblical truth that Jesus and the apostles were intentionally focused on developing maturity, and the contemporary church mostly isn't, it shouldn't come as a surprise that many members aren't able to withstand the pressures, temptations, and suffering found within the ministry and throughout life.

I end this chapter with an interesting dichotomy: on the one hand I would argue for a fresh urgency for the development of maturity within the church; but on the other hand I would argue that time should be taken and the process not rushed. If both tenets of this dichotomy hold true, then the correct mindset with which to approach every new believer that walks into the Kingdom would be the following: 'It is going to take me a couple of years to bring this person to maturity, so I better be focused and not waste any time.'

DISCERNMENT

Hebrews 5:14 (ESV) But solid food is for the mature, for those who have their powers of discernment trained by constant practice to distinguish good from evil.

It is the responsibility of the mature believer to distinguish between good and evil. As with Jesus, the mature believer should ideally not have to be told, taught, led by the hand, instructed, guided, admonished, coerced, or receive any other form of assistance when it comes to the distinguishing between good and evil. How starkly this contrasts with the contemporary church experience of looking to the leader, or the elder, or the mentor for moral guidance? This is not to say that there will never be a season or times in which the mature believer looks to another for assistance. The Scripture, however, is clear: the mature believer has undergone a process of constant practice in which they have developed the ability to accurately discern by and for themselves.

Consider for a moment the implication of this scripture on discipleship strategy. A sound discipleship strategy should at some stage migrate from consistent moral instruction or guidance, to that of coaching. What is the difference one might ask? Think of it in the same manner as a person learning a new sport or board game. Initially one needs to teach them the rules and tactics. However, after that initial investment they need to start playing and making decisions for themselves. The coach now stands back and lets them pray, think, and act by themselves. Wins, losses, and injuries are part and parcel of the process, and feedback is now provided during the breaks or in between games. The key to understand is that during the game, the player is responsible for his or her own decisions and actions. They have been trained and empowered to make their own decisions whilst the clock is running.

In this same way, yes, there will be a season where the mentor, or pastor, or leader, or whichever role the senior person finds themselves in, constantly tells the receiver what they should or should not be doing. This is what we have to do for infants to keep them safe. As the believer grows, however, the senior person needs to stand back and encourage them to make their own decisions. The game of life needs to be played without constant interference from the coach. Yes, the coach is available when apt or needed, but the responsibility for playing lies with the believer. Otherwise, you will end up not with a mature believer, but rather an adult child.

Furthermore, the strategy of dialogue between the coach and the player also becomes important. A bad coach always blusters forth: you should do this, you should do that, you should have done this, you should have done that. A good coach asks questions: why did you do this? What was your thinking? Were there other options? What does Scripture or the Spirit say in this or that regard? Why didn't you follow that? Depending on the answers, the good coach will give feedback and assist the player in becoming a more mindful and mature player.

As I'm writing this, I hear the chorus of pastoral voices in my ears, 'But that's what we're doing!' At the risk of offending many of the readers I humbly offer this observation: most pastors talk too much. It's understandable, though. The Scriptural mandate is that one should be sent to preach and that elders should be able to teach, so it comes with the territory. Furthermore, most pastors that I've had to do with are also quite serious about their calling (yes, I've unfortunately also met some that'll rather be on the golf or tennis court than with their members). These serious pastors see it as their Godly responsibility to impart and invest. However, most still talk too much, and in the talking they take up the discernment responsibilities of their members and sadly bind them into a state of perpetual infancy.

Believers need to be allowed and encouraged to discern for themselves what is good and evil.

All of this assumes that, during the infancy phase, they were taught the correct tools: sound doctrine (clearly laid out by the writer of Hebrews), basic Scriptural study methods, how to pray and receive accurate Word from the Spirit, and how to employ the gift of discernment. In a world reluctant to use the word 'evil', clear delineation between good and evil needs to be provided, otherwise how will they identify which is which? This necessitates, and we will touch on it in the next chapter, that the believer has a clear understanding of God's character and the nature of morality within the Kingdom of God. The believer needs to look at data— meaning, an incident, circumstances, dialogue, etc.— and know that this, or that, is not of God.

This should impress on the reader that a focused preparatory path is critical to the believer's long term survival. Church leadership will, at most, see their congregation members for a couple of short sessions a week. Most of these sessions won't be personal in nature. For the rest of the week the believer will find themselves in a hostile and dangerous world, with an enemy waiting to pounce and devour them. How on earth can we think they'll survive if they are not able to function on their own? The whole purpose of the fivefold ministry is to facilitate this preparation, and the cornerstone of this preparation is the ability of the believer to spot the lion stalking them from the bush.

In the same way, how do we expect the believer to navigate complex decisions? Or avoid traps and pitfalls set them by the enemy's agents? 'But they must study more Bible,' I hear some of you say. Yes, we can all do with more of the Word in our lives, but the writer in Hebrew is much more specific: the mature are those who have had their powers of discernment trained by constant practice to distinguish good from evil. My argument, very strongly, is that we reconsider our somewhat lackadaisical, and sadly almost cliche, approach to disciplines like praying and reading our Bibles, and instead start teaching and impressing on believers how to use those tools to discern between good and evil.

Take an active approach in empowering believers to discern for themselves, and we find a massive benefit arising. When the infant believer has been taught, and the elders always need to ask themselves whether they've correctly done their part, but when the infant believer in fact has been taught on a matter, and they still choose less than ideally, it grants insight into their hearts. Now the coach can change the line of questioning, 'Listen, I know you've been taught on this. I know you understand which option was the good and Godly one, but you still picked wrong. What's up with that? What's happening in your heart? Are you really serious about this matter?' This type of confrontation might make some uncomfortable. However, I suggest we lay our fear of man aside and rather concern ourselves with believers' growth and maturity.

If I was a betting man, I would put my money on the following (and feel free to try it): if we had to approach our congregation members and ask them the following two questions, 'Hey, are you well practiced in your ability to discern good from evil? Can you teach me how to do it as well?' We would be shocked (or maybe not) to find most of them blustering through the answers. As a member of the Body of Christ, one that's both committed to and deeply respectful of the church, I am terribly concerned about the fact that we are not teaching people this skill. Apart from the Biblical revelation that it is a cornerstone of spiritual maturity, it keeps me up at night that believers are trying to navigate the world without the ability to, or even the understanding that they should, be able to accurately discern good from evil. Lord, help us that we are not literally throwing our members to the wolves.

LIBERTY

Galatians 5:1 (ESV) For freedom Christ has set us free; stand firm therefore, and do not submit again to a yoke of slavery.

As with developing maturity, the contemporary church seems somewhat confused in its approach to sin. Frequently, the laying down of sin is also projected as a 'lifelong endeavor' instead of a task to be completed as fast as possible. Again, due to sin being present in our bodies, and the reality of an enemy that wants to destroy us, we will be confronted with temptation until the day we die. The Scriptural intention, however, is not to say that we cannot or should not walk in victory sooner rather than later.

We seem to forget, or misunderstand, that dealing with sin is not the endgame. Dealing with sin, in the same way as developing maturity, is a preparatory action. We are supposed to delve into both and get them sorted out (at least to some degree), so that we might move on to other things. Lifelong fruitful ministry, that is to say, effectiveness in the Kingdom of God, is built on a holy, free, and mature foundation. As such, sin should be dealt with quickly and aggressively.

One might consider reframing the issue of sin within the context of liberty. It is the free man or woman that is able to give their all to Jesus. Conversely, those bound by sin will always have parts of themselves, as well as certain of their resources, held back from Christ. The journey in dealing with sin is essentially the process of becoming fully free children of God.

Let me make a somewhat controversial statement: God is not concerned about what is right and wrong. The fundamentalist compartments of right and wrong, as an independent and arbitrary judge of righteousness, is a man made construct. The morality of Scripture is not rooted in abstract rightness and wrongness, but rather in God's own character.

In Exodus 33:18-22, when Moses asks God to show him His presence, God indicates that it's His goodness that will pass before the prophet. The main descriptor of God's character is good. Not as in 'a nice guy,' but good as in contrast with evil. God is a good God. Christian morality then is rooted within the understanding of what is good and what is evil. This is why we are called to discern between good and evil, not right and wrong.

All other attributes of God is conjoined with that basic goodness. He is life, He is pure, He is wise, He is honest and transparent. Where His Spirit is there is freedom. These are the things God is concerned with, and our morality is rooted within these character elements of who and what God is. A sinful desire, action, or habit isn't sinful because it is wrong; it is sinful because it's evil, leads to death, is impure, is foolish, leads to willful deceit, and is binding. This is why sin is 'hamartia'— Greek for 'missing the mark'.

Why is it important to consider this approach? Let me first assure you that it's not some postmodern deconstruction of the term 'sin'. There are certain desires, actions, and habits that are difficult to identify as sinful when approaching them from the paradigm of 'right and wrong'. Some might argue that, 'No! Scripture has an answer for everything!' Yes, in principle, but Scripture doesn't speak directly to coffee or prescription medicine addiction, or to the consumption of certain types of media, or how we use technology in contemporary society. This is precisely why we need to be training our members to discern what is good and what is evil. Christians need to own the ability to evaluate any and all desires, thoughts, actions, and habits in the light of God's goodness. This is the road to maturity. It is the infant that needs to be told what to do, not the mature adult.

It might also be helpful to differentiate between regular and persistent sin. There were sinful practices which we were easily able to lay down, and then there were or are sinful practices that we have struggled to lay down. Each and every Christian can attest to this reality.

Regular sin is easy to deal with: if there's sincere repentance it's simply and act of laying it down through the Spirit and then stopping it. Christ, through the Spirit, has granted us this grace and we should not make light of it. If we are able to stop it, then we should stop it. Scripture frequently uses the term 'uproot'. It denotes taking a weed by its roots and plucking it out. This is our responsibility when it comes to regular sin.

What about persistent sin? Do we have permission to simply carry on with it? Does grace cover it in perpetuity? Whereas the extension of grace is God's personal prerogative, Scripture mandates us to deal with persistent sin as we would with any other type of sin. This, partly, is why I would argue that a period of maturing is required in the first place: so that we might deal with persistent sin before bearing the terrible weight of responsibility.

Another way of approaching the issue of regular or persistent sin is to consider whether it has a binding root. Regular sin, most frequently, is simply a pattern of thoughts and/or actions that one has adopted at some stage during one's life. The spiritual order of things is that the Spirit would shed light on that thought, action, or habit, revealing it as sinful to the believer, and the believer can simply lay it down. You might imagine the believer thinking, 'Ah, this is sinful, and I should not be doing it,' and then stopping it. Persistent sin is not as simple.

With persistent sin the process of revelation would be the same. However, this time round, the believer might have one of two responses: first, imagine the believer thinking, 'Mmmm, I'm not so sure whether I really want to stop this,' and the sin continues; or second, imagine the believer thinking, 'Ah, this is sinful, and I should not be doing it,' but irrespective of how hard they try to lay it down, the sin continues.

Let's tackle the first case. James teaches us that the origin of sinful actions are our sinful desires. It is a cascading process that starts from desires, and then leads to thoughts, decisions, habits, and eventual death. It should stand to reason that we need to deal with the desires, if and when they are present, before we can deal with the actions. Sadly, few believers have been taught this. It's tragic, though, as most times when one uproots the desires (or lays them down by the Spirit), the sinful actions disappear by themselves. Our first question then, when dealing with persistent sin, should be, 'Are you sincere in the fact that you want to stop this? Do you really and deeply want to? Or are you only trying to stop because of external pressure?' Knowing one should stop a sinful practice, and deeply wanting to, are two wholly different things. God ignores the first and empowers the second.

Unfortunately we can't stop there. There are believers that deeply desire to stop with sinful practices but still don't attain freedom. At the root of this most persistent type of sin, almost without exception, lies trauma. Not only Trauma with a capital 'T' — think being raped, or losing a parent when young, or medical or financial crises — but frequently also trauma with a lower case 't'. What is this you may ask? We forget that we live in an exceptionally toxic culture. The sinful degradation of society has led us to a place where very few humans make it to adulthood without significant damage to their souls.

Trauma with a lowercase 't' is the accumulation—the emotional scar tissue—of each and every act of hurt and destruction that has been sown into the life of a person. When persistent sin passes the desire check, look for trauma. What we are seeing as evil sin (and it might very well be evil in effect, if not root) is frequently the coping or defense mechanism of a broken person. Truly healthy and resilient people don't need coping or defense mechanisms, and so they don't display as much persistent sin.

A surefire strategy to dealing with sin arises: pursue liberty in all things. Liberty from regular sin, liberty from sinful desires, and liberty from trauma.

It would do us well to recap a principle from the start of the chapter. We are called to deal with sin and to mature so that we might become effective within the Kingdom. Much damage has been done to the church and the Kingdom by granting responsibility to those that have not dealt with persistent sin.

Again, I lay this failure not at the feet of the new convert, but at the feet of myself and my fellow elders. Our focus and relationship with our church members should be such that we are helping them deal with sin. We need to be talking about it. I'm not proposing a sin–consciousness, where we all buckle under the guilt and shame of all our transgressions, but the old adage is true: the church that doesn't talk about sin is the church that loses to sin. Is your church still talking about sin? And are you still talking to your mentees and disciples about their sin?

Are you guiding your members and mentees through the practices of identifying, uprooting, and/or laying down of sin? If you desire spiritually mature believers, members that are stable and consistent both in attendance and service, then you need to help them deal with sin.

OBEDIENCE

1 Corinthians 2:14 (ESV) The natural person does not accept the things of the Spirit of God, for they are folly to him, and he is not able to understand them because they are spiritually discerned.

1 Corinthians 3:1-3 (ESV) 1 But I, brothers, could not address you as spiritual people, but as people of the flesh, as infants in Christ. 2 I fed you with milk, not solid food, for you were not ready for it. And even now you are not yet ready, 3 for you are still of the flesh. For while there is jealousy and strife among you, are you not of the flesh and behaving only in a human way?

Natural, fleshly, and spiritual. These are the categories into which Paul divides all persons at any given time. The natural man, the person who's spirit has not been quickened to life, as per Ephesians 2:5, is simply not able to accept the things of the Spirit. This means that the natural man will have inherent struggles in understanding, discerning, and/or being obedient to those things that are of and from Jesus. For the natural man, the problem is one of capability. That is to say, he or she lacks the Spirit by which they can consistently draw from, or lean on, throughout their life–journey.

The person of the flesh does not have that problem. The person of the flesh has been quickened to life and has full access to God's grace through the inhabitation of the Holy Spirit. The Spirit is permanently within them and has committed Himself to their assistance and empowerment. The fleshly believer has the ever–present option to engage the Holy Spirit but, for whatever reason, does not.

It's important to state that the categories differ somewhat qualitatively: being natural is a permanent state of being until the day one's spirit is enlivened by God; being fleshly versus spiritual is a state of flux for each and every born again believer. A person does not go from natural, to fleshly, to spiritual, like one would go from one, to two, to three. One goes from natural, to a state where one struggles between flesh and spirit. Even the most mature believer may occasionally act according to the flesh, but they will not become natural again. It is the process of being and acting more consistently spiritual, rather than fleshly, which one calls maturing. The mature man or woman of God is the more spiritual and less fleshly man or woman.

But what does that mean, to be spiritual? It's quite simple: the spiritual person is the one which is obedient to God. If, in the moment, one discerns something to be avoided due to it being destructive, and one avoids it through the empowering of the Spirit, then one has acted spiritually. If one discerns the need to avoid this thing but doesn't, then one has acted according to the flesh. The same applies to the opposite: if one discerns an action that should be taken, and one does, then one has acted spiritually.

To be spiritual is not a feature of being charismatic, having visions, being swept into certain states of being, bursting out in laughing or tongues, or any of the myriad displays of contemporary 'spirituality', to be spiritual is simply to be obedient. Paraphrasing for emphasis: if you want to be the most spiritual person in the building, you would need to become the most obedient person in the building.

Obviously, this necessitates that the language of obedience, in conjunction with discernment, is used. New believers should be taught, from the start, or at least from as soon as possible, that they now enter a life in which they should consistently discern good from evil, followed by applying themselves to become more and more obedient to the leading that they experience. This means that they need to be both proficient and disciplined in this regard. As per the chapter on 'Discernment', the new believer needs to be equipped with the skills for discernment. As per the chapter on 'Liberty' the new believer needs to receive the correct doctrinal foundation with which to support this skill.

In conjunction with these, they need to be discipled into becoming obedient. In Mathew 28:20, Jesus sends out His apostles with the explicit command, paraphrased here, to teach believers to obey His teachings.

Again I note the seeming confusion in the church: the fivefold ministry is not called to teach for teaching's sake, they are called to bring believers to obedience. The goal of the teaching should not be presentation of information, but rather the stimulation of transformation. Whatever the platform God has given us, whether pulpit, Sunday school class, small group, or one–on–one discipleship, our approach and methods should be such that we are actively pressing the believer to become more obedient. As we have already seen, this is not an issue of telling the believer what he or she should do, but rather helping them identify why they were or are not being obedient in the first place.

Interestingly, all of this stands in stark contrast with the elegant and creative motivational–speeches we receive from many contemporary pulpits. Consider Paul: he says that when he came to speak it was not with the plausible words of wisdom, but with a demonstration of power and Spirit. Incidentally, I'm not relieving those with a teaching ministry from being good communicators. Jesus, Paul, Peter, James, the list goes on, were obviously all skilled and well rounded orators. Their focus, however, was not on being elegant and entertaining, and they were not info–dumping either—they were laser focused on bringing forth transformation.

Well, how does that work, you might ask? Transformation is an interplay between revelation and obedience. For transformation to be affected a Biblical truth first needs to be revealed to the believer. This can be through many vectors but, as we have learned earlier, the believer should not have to be spoon fed, or milk–fed, for the rest of their lives. Teaching, praying, Bible study, mentorship, discernment in the moment, all of these and more address the revelation part of the equation. And the obedience part of the equation? One word: submission. It's critical to understand, though, that submission is an active employment of the will. A person's will does not automatically submit to a revelation, if that was the case humans would not be free. No, we have a free will, and that means that for a person to submit to a revelation, they need to actively employ their will.

In short, they need to make a decision. The will has to go through the actual process of, 'I choose this or that.'

Furthermore, the decision is not to be fleshly, or of the person. Instead, the decision needs to be driven both by the Spirit's revelation as well as the Spirit's empowerment. It is by the Spirit that we should choose this or that, and do this or that. On a practical level, there is value in literally praying, choosing, thinking, and speaking in this manner. We don't have to hope for the best, we can draw on the Holy Spirit to empower our decisions. 'I choose this,' can become, 'By the Spirit of God, I choose this' or possibly, 'Holy Spirit please empower this choice.' Rather than getting hung up on methods, remember what we are trying to achieve: the believer needs to understand that active decision making is necessary and that it should be done in conjunction with the Spirit's leading and empowering.

An interesting question might be this: where do you allow for that active participation of the will? Is there intentional prompting and space, whether in your prayer, talking, teaching, or ministry, in which the receiver can take the time to employ their will? Incidentally, this is the foundation of altar and any other type of call during or after services. It provides the believer with the opportunity to respond to the revelation they have received.

Does this mean we require an altar call after each and every service? No, most definitely not. However, I would strongly argue for a 'transformative opportunity' in each and every get together—irrespective of the size or type of gathering. More specifically, this 'transformative opportunity' should be well led and guided by whoever's leading. I'm not suggesting that the minister be prescriptive and tell the receiver what to do, but simply that he or she creates the time and space in which the receiver can be invited to engage and respond to the Holy Spirit, and then that the minister would step back and let the Spirit do the work. It is Him, ultimately, that brings forth the transformation, not our plausible words as Paul calls them. A fresh vision for all our teaching might be this: our teaching is a setup for Him to do His work. We teach only to guide the believer to understanding, and then we create some time and space, stand back, and let the receiver work it out with God.

As the believer matures, as their will is trained, their submission will become quicker, easier, and require less prompting from their teacher. Sadly, many believers' growth is stilted because they are not taught the act of submission, they are not provided with the space in which to do so, and so they are never actively developed into becoming disciplined and obedient followers of Christ.

You can change this.

TRAINING

Hebrews 5:14 (ESV) But solid food is for the mature, for those who have their powers of discernment trained by constant practice to distinguish good from evil.

Ephesians 4:11-13 (ESV) 11 And he gave the apostles, the prophets, the evangelists, the shepherds and teachers, 12 to equip the saints for the work of ministry, for building up the body of Christ, 13 until we all attain to the unity of the faith and of the knowledge of the Son of God, to mature manhood, to the measure of the stature of the fullness of Christ,

Matthew 28:19-20 (ESV) 19 Go therefore and make disciples of all nations, baptizing them in the name of the Father and of the Son and of the Holy Spirit, 20 teaching them to observe all that I have commanded you. And behold, I am with you always, to the end of the age."

It should be evident, by this time, that maturity is developed intentionally. It is not something that can be left to chance. Furthermore, we should be warned away from the ludicrous idea that maturity will somehow develop organically if we just hope and pray enough; Jesus, Paul, and the writer of Hebrews all show an intentional focus on the development of maturity. As with many other things, our co–working with Christ should be displayed throughout the process of maturing, whether in ourselves and others. That is to say, we have an active role to play in the matter, we have been tasked by Jesus to teach others to 'observe all' that He has commanded us and to do so ourselves.

How might this look? Before we get to that, let me highlight the issue of 'church programs'. I am South African. We always tease that whenever our government wants to do anything, they first establish a committee. In this same manner, it seems like whenever the contemporary church wants to do anything, they start a new program. Obviously there's nothing inherently wrong with church programs, as they allow you to focus on certain content and outcomes, but conversely, it's not as if church programs have been a silver bullet either. Also, have you noticed that church programs, as we know them, are conspicuously missing from Scripture? I'm very hesitant to say that we need some program or the other with which to tackle the issue of maturity.

Instead, this Little Book proposes that we need a fresh focus. With a fresh focus will come fresh dialogue, fresh thinking, and fresh practice. In short, all the elements of a refreshed and reawakened culture will follow—if we are able to change our focus. As such, it's irrelevant whether we use discipleship groups, small groups, or service platforms to work our ways toward maturity. Scripture, by the way, shows a healthy community as including all of these. Am I contradicting myself? No, I'm trying to communicate that launching a new type of group program is not the point, rather, the point is what is the focus of those groups when they come together.

A new focus also doesn't necessitate new content (although it might). Meaning, we don't have to go Google for the best 'small group maturity program', or 'preaching topics that lead to maturity', or 'xxxxxx church network's discipleship program'. It's not the focus of this treatment, but I could strongly argue that the church should move away from this mindset: it is not Scripturally mandated or evidenced.

A new focus is just that: a new focus. It's going to Jesus and responding to the call to maturity. Submitting our own will to this call, as and while we bring others to this same submission. Suddenly, as with other points of growth, new conversations will start to flow around the topic. Believers will become more aware that such a thing as spiritual maturity exists and that it is to be desired and pursued.

This talking, like the rudder of a ship, will have an effect on thinking, aspirations, and planning. New praxis can follow: as we all come to understand that we are called to spiritual maturity, having conversations about discernment, liberty, and obedience will become more and more comfortable.

The next important factor is to understand the requirements of spiritual maturity as set out in Scripture. This Little Book provides insight into certain key dynamics whilst purposefully staying away from the doctrinal foundation that each and every believer needs to attain (see Hebrews 6:1-6). The church has long ago mastered doctrinal teaching and I'm hesitant to digress in that direction. For that reason, let us rather return to the somewhat forgotten elements as highlighted in this treatment.

Paul notes in Ephesians, that amongst other things, the fivefold ministry is called to equip the saints for the works of the ministry, with the goal of bringing them to maturity. Equipping presupposes training. This accords with Hebrews, showing us that our powers of discernment is trained through constant practice. Note that the concepts of 'equipping', 'training', and 'practice' all denote an active participation by the recipient. If you should go to any vocational school, sports academy, or arts class, you will see training: students are taught how to do something, and then they have to do it. This process is repeated consistently, with a teacher or instructor acting as a coach. In other words, the skill is practiced until mastered.

Maturity is not an issue of knowledge alone, but of skill and discipline layered on top of knowledge. The ability to discern is a skill that should be practiced and employed in a disciplined manner. Yes, knowledge plays a formative part, but only in the same way that a rugby player's knowledge of the rules of the game does; whether the rugby player plays for his country is a matter of skill through discipline. Obedience on the other hand, is less of a skill and more of a general practice, albeit one that also requires discipline in execution. Both will initially require some knowledge based training, but they are only ever mastered through consistent practice.

All of this should impress upon the reader that a certain amount of effort is required to become mature. It doesn't just happen. Learning takes effort, practices takes effort, becoming a disciplined person takes effort. Incidentally, this is not to say that we are falling back into dead works; this topic has nothing to do with our salvation. Simply use common sense: if I am to discern between good and evil, for example, it means that I need to stop, take the time that is needed, and apply myself to the act of discernment. This is effort. Luckily, by the grace of God, if we are disciplined in our practice then this process eventually becomes reactionary (a technical term for what some would call habitual).

We circle back to the issue of focus. If we want to develop maturity in the Body of Christ, then we need to create opportunities for members to practice their discernment and obedience under the care of other mature believers. The question then is simple: where in the platforms that we have do we do this? Where is the opportunity for discernment and obedience in the discipleship group? What does that opportunity look like? Where is that opportunity in the small group? And where is it in the larger service? Some detractors would say, 'No, only the educated and ordained can minister in those spaces.' To which I say, 'Be careful, for it is the Spirit of God who ministers through us all.' The actual issue here is not whether some should be allowed to actively participate (I invite you to review 1Cor 14:26 in any case), but whether that participation is done in a manner that promotes growth and safeguard's the flock. In a nutshell, it simply needs to be managed by the elders.

Am I proposing an 'open mic' approach to services? Not necessarily, no. What I'm saying is that training, practice, and participation, especially in the acts of discernment and obedience, should be fostered within ALL spaces where the church comes together. In this way, the believer will be discipled into deeply understanding that they can discern the leading of the Spirit, and that they should be obedient to that leading, wherever they might find themselves. Furthermore, this freedom to practice under the oversight and loving correction of mature believers is crucial in working out the kinks. It is the mature believer that'll know when the young believer is talking or acting out of concert with the Word and Spirit. This is God's way: that the immature might learn and practice under the mature's guidance.

The only question that matters is where and how do we allow and foster this training and practice when we come together.

READINESS

A healthy church culture is one where active service opportunities are available at all times. Believers, whether young or old, man or woman, immature or mature, should be able to slot in and be trained up in the works of the ministry, My assumption is that the reader understands that this relates to more than just packing chairs and washing dishes. How does one learn discernment between good and evil when packing chairs? Or, for that matter, how does one sharpen one's obedience when it comes to drying off the coffee cups? No, the works of the ministry relate to all the gifts of grace and the Spirit that the Body has received, and a maturity focused church offers opportunities for members to practice these under the guidance of the elders and other mature believers.

This guided practice, incidentally, is the safety net against inexperience. Again leaving methods up to the reader, what's important is that an elder or a mature believer is able to discern and identify when the trainee is going off point. Many of you would know that when we start practicing our gifts we are initially guilty of misinterpretations, acts of sinful commission, and acts of sinful omission. In layman's terms: we get things wrong, say and do too much, and say and do too little. We are still learning how to be precise; we are still developing our ability to discern with a very high level of accuracy and consistency and to be obedient to that leading. It is the work of the mature believer, or the elder, to lovingly realign us when we miss it.

Unfortunately, due to a wide range of reasons, many churches have no active spaces in which the immature can practice these skills. There are teaching spaces but, sadly, very little practice spaces. In this way, we keep our members bound to immaturity, and then we wonder why they never become the stable and consistent believers we so desperately need.

This chapter, however, concerns readiness. It concerns the question: when is the believer ready? Well, when it comes to active service under the guidance of the mature, the answer is immediately and always. If a person has truly been born again, the Spirit of God will press them into a new vision for life, with much energy and drive accompanying that new vision. This person is ready to learn and ready to practice.

'That's easier said than done!' I hear the detractors shout. 'We have many teams and small groups but they don't want to commit!' No, each and every believer won't commit. However, my analytical mind would like to ask you whether we're talking about new converts or existing believers? Methods aside, my experience is that these two categories frequently need a different approach. New converts, and I'm thinking about myself and many others throughout my ministry career, tend to be more open to involvement. If their conversion is sincere and authentic, then the Spirit will drive them to get involved. If we don't embrace and disciple them according to Scripture, well, that's on us. In contrast, when it comes to existing believers, a sound strategy and a lot of prayer is usually required to turn the tide in the direction of seeking maturity.

Furthermore, if you've been following my arguments, I'm not necessarily proposing trying to funnel every member into some team or the other. For various reasons that fall outside the scope of this treatment, people are hesitant to commit to groups or teams. Many of these reasons aren't inherently lazy or evil, sometimes it might be as simple as time or capacity constraints. The problem, though, is this: if we have relegated all ministry training and practice to groups, programs, and teams, what about the rest that aren't active in those spaces? Are we comfortable leaving the bulk of our congregations in a state of infancy solely because they can't or don't want to commit to a prescribed space? My argument, based on Scriptural evidence, is that training should happen in all communal spaces; the Bible does not show any evidence of relegated 'training spaces'.

To close off this point: anecdotal arguments against the Scriptural mandate to have believers practice when they come together are moot. I've heard too many stories of church members being denied the opportunity to practice their gifts (in gatherings of all sizes), due to them being inaccurate and potentially causing harm. This is the whole point of having a mature contingent of believers guiding the immature. If your immature believers are causing harm, it's because your mature believers are not up to scratch. If your mature believers are not up to scratch then it means your elders (which include the presiding pastor) don't know what they are doing. The old adage rings true: each and every church gets the culture that the elders deserve.

I summarise: under the guidance of the mature, believers are at all times ready for active service and ministry.

Our next question is when is the believer ready for responsibility. What is responsibility in the church, btw? It is when a believer is appointed, positionally or hierarchically, with tending to certain people or outcomes. They have to 'make things happen'. Whether shepherding, leading, or administrating, and whether in discipleship groups, small groups, are service assemblies, there is a buck that stops with that person. Results are expected, feedback will be required, instructions will be given. For practical purposes think pastors, team and small group leaders, teachers and other forms of appointed ministers, worship leaders, highly visible and very prominent teams and team member. Essentially any person that forms a key role in the church.

In the spiritual realm, any and all of these persons will experience an extra measure of pressure when they step into a role of responsibility. This pressure has three main points of origin.

First, we seem to forget that we are in a constant spiritual battle. There is an enemy. That enemy has agents with the clear intention of destroying humans and the church. They will target you, tempt you, set you up, outsmart you whenever they can, and basically use every opportunity available to try and get you to fail and be disqualified from the church or ministry.

Second, most of the world currently lives in a toxic culture that places immense demands on individual capacity. People are constantly struggling with their energy levels, as well as their psychological and physical health; lack of resiliency is a very real problem.

Third, there is a moral demand placed on any person that assumes any form of responsibility in the church. Irrespective of the level of maturity that a believer reaches, they will always be held to a higher moral standard than those around them. This reality brings its own pressures with it: you have to be careful, you have to watch your step, you have to place others' interests above your own, you have to humble yourself frequently. None of these come easily for the flesh.

So this is what happens when we haven't done the work, and we take our 'very nice and consistently attending church member', and give them a small group to lead: we take a potentially damaged, tired, and un–resilient human being, and we expose them to tremendous moral, demonic, and capacity drains. And then six months, or two years down the line, we wonder why their character failed or why they suffered burnout.

So when is a believer ready for responsibility in the church? When they have reached an adequate level of maturity. That is to say, when they have reached a place of stability and consistency, not in the natural due to their temperament type, but in the spiritual. This means that they would have reached a certain level of healing, that their lives reflect the habits that pertain to capacity and resiliency, and that they are accurate in the spirit and that they have trained their will to obedience. None of this will guarantee a ministry term free of mistakes and missteps, but it should guarantee a ministry term that's well run and well finished.

THE STORY BEHIND THE STORY

In 2022, I suffered a severe injury and was forced to resign from a successful career as instructor and operator in certain specialised security and law enforcement environments. My wife and I had long been sensing that a change in career was due, but it never occurred to us that it would happen through a catastrophe!

In any case, some of you might know that before the medically induced retirement, I was both a traditionally and self published author in two nonfiction fields. I've been writing for some time (first published in 2015), and after the dust settled (said dust including being blind a couple of times, offloading two successful businesses, quitting my teams, three surgeries, and four months of discomfort and being mostly housebound), it made sense to at least try and continue with the writing. However, instead of focusing purely on nonfiction, the decision was made to also venture into a career as independent novelist.

Probably the most unexpected part of this journey was to discover that I immensely enjoy writing full time. Up until the injury, I was a career professional that also wrote. Now, I am a writer, and I am deeply thankful that I have found this career path after what was essentially a life altering tragedy.

From my side, you have my commitment that I will always strive to master my craft. Know that I care deeply about each one of you, and that my respect for you has me working hard at each and every next project!

From your side, if you have the time and inclination, you can support me in this journey by leaving a small review of this book on your platform of choice. Simply search for the platform online, alongside my name, surname, and the book title, and navigate over to the reviews section.

Reviews not only help me sell more books—which essentially allows me to do this full time—but also gives me insight into your thoughts concerning my work.

A humble and sincere 'thank you' in advance!

SOCIAL MEDIA LINKS

You can follow me on my social media channels—and please do check in! I sincerely enjoy connecting with my readers.

www.facebook.com/schalkhollowayauthor
www.instagram.com/schalkhollowayauthor

Schalk is a published author, lay minister and retired professional instructor and special operations response team leader with 18 years experience running interventions in at-risk communities and 7 years experience executing urban tactical and intelligence based operations.

www.ingramcontent.com/pod-product-compliance
Lightning Source LLC
Chambersburg PA
CBHW061628130726
47996CB00003B/1166